THE CHINESE MENU COOKBOOK
for the Family & Dinner Party

THE CHINESE MENU COOKBOOK

for the Family & Dinner Party

Constance D. Chang

Shufunotomo Co., Ltd.

Revised Edition
First printing, 1988

Published by SHUFUNOTOMO CO., LTD.
2-9, Kanda Surugadai, Chiyoda-ku, Tokyo, 101 Japan

ISBN: 4-07-974794-2
Printed in Japan

Preface

To my dear Readers:
Since 1951 I have written 14 Chinese cookbooks and taught Chinese cooking in classes and on TV programs. The books have been published in Hongkong, Tokyo, London, New York, San Francisco and Hawaii. Some of them were also translated into German, Dutch and Portuguese.

This volume, "The Chinese Menu Cookbook- for the Family and Dinner Party" presents basic principles of Chinese menus applicable both to ordering in a restaurant as well as to cooking in your own kitchen. The first six groups of recipes suggest menus consisting of five courses each to serve four to six persons. The recipes are simple and easy to follow with step-by-step illustrations. All ingredients are available at any supermarket (fresh ones are always preferable to frozen ones) and no special kitchen utensils are required.

These recipes are interchangeable as shown below, and may be combined to make as many as 150 assorted menus:

A	B	C	D	E	F	—	A	B	C	D	E	F	—
1	1	1	1	1	1	—	A1	B1	C1	A1	D1	F1	—
2	2	2	2	2	2	—	B2	E2	E2	C2	F2	E2	—
3	3	3	3	3	3	—	C3	C3	B3	E3	D3	B3	—
4	4	4	4	4	4	—	D4	F4	F4	B4	A4	A4	—
5	5	5	5	5	5	—	E5	D5	D5	F5	C5	A5	—

and so on.

The simplest Chinese meal consists of one soup and one dish served with steamed rice, when one is eating alone.

The regular meal at home consists of four or five dishes. The suggested menus given in this book can be used for the family or for small dinner parties. The Chinese menu emphasizes variety; for instance, varieties in the following categories:

1) ingredients (i.e., vegetables, pork, beef, seafood, etc.)
2) ways of cooking (i.e., steaming, boiling, sauté (stir-frying), stewing, deep-frying, etc.)
3) ways of cutting (i.e., slicing, dicing, shredding, oblique-cutting, cutting in chunks, etc.)
4) flavoring (i.e., salt, garlic, chili, soy sauce, sugar, vinegar, etc.)

A balanced meal of five dishes must consist of one meat, one vegetable, one seafood, one soup and one dessert. If you want to add one more dish, perhaps you can have one dish of fried noodles or fried rice, or any meat or vegatables. For example, take menu E on page xx.

	1	2	3	4
E1	Soup (Won Ton)	boiling	minced meat	salt
E2	Vegetable (eggplant)	sauté	slicing lengthwise	garlic
E3	Seafood (shrimp)	stewed	n/a	chili
E4	Chicken	deep-frying	chunks	soy sauce
E5	Dessert (orange)	heating	juice	sugar

Chinese cooking is considered an art; each dish, therefore, should be well prepared to delight the senses. According to the Chinese saying, there are 3 important condition—" 色 " color—for the eyes, " 香 " aroma—for the nose, and " 味 " taste—for the mouth. It is more fun to cook for others—friends, colleagues in the office, relatives, or visitors from other places, than just for oneself.

This cookbook offers many special suggestions for home parties, from Chinese-style light snacks and pastries to full dinners for different occasions. If you want more servings you can double each recipe as you desire.

The Chinese people are well-known for their hospitality. Everyone is obliged to give a party for some reason, at one time or another, and many people simply enjoy entertaining. To entertain at a restaurant is too unimaginative and could be very expensive. You can avoid such unnecessary expenses. If you entertain at home with your own cooking, the party will be one that is long remembered and more sincerely enjoyed by your guests. I hope you will find in this book the skill and the confidence to prepare Chinese food for your guests. Since you do not have the opportunity to watch my TV program and are not able to join my cooking classes in Japan, I invite you to try the simple recipes in this book. The results will look the same as those in the color pictures, and will taste delicious too.

By using this book as a reference, I am sure that you will be able to plan and cook authentic Chinese menus, as well as place orders in a Chinese restaurant.

Constance D. Chang

Contents

FAMILY MENUS A TO F

Directions

1. Recipes from each menu are interchangeable and may be combined to make an infinite number of assorted menus.
2. Each menu serves 4 to 6 persons.
3. Unless otherwise specified, vegetable oil is used for frying, and the dishes are to be served hot.
4. Hints and suggestions on table setting and for hors d'oeuvre and beverages are given on pages 102–104.

FAMILY MENUS
A TO F

MENU A

1. Tomato Clam Soup
2. Deep-Fried
   Walnut Chicken
3. Sweet-Sour Pork
4. Cucumber Salad
5. Egg Fried Rice

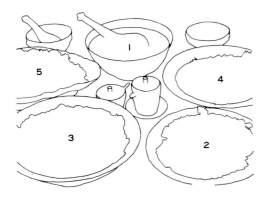

MENU A-1 蕃茄蛤肉湯

TOMATO CLAM SOUP

OVER MEDIUM HEAT

Ingredients:
3 dozen small-sized clams, unshucked
4 tomatoes (about 1½ lb., 750 g)
5 cups chicken stock
1 tablespoon scallion, diced diagonally
3 tablespoons oil
½ teaspoon pepper
1–1½ teaspoons salt
1½ tablespoons cornstarch dissolved in 3 tablespoons water
Salad or sesame oil

Method:
1. Boil clams in 2½ cups of water until shells open, pick out meat and wash away sand.

2. Blanch tomatoes for half a minute, peel off skin and cut into 6 or 8 wedges.

3. Heat oil and fry tomato pieces until soft. Strain, using a piece of clean gauze or a sieve, and discard pulp. To tomato, add chicken stock, clams, pepper and salt. Cook for 2 minutes. Add scallion and dissolved cornstarch. Stir until boiling and sprinkle a dash of salad or sesame oil on surface. Serve in a warmed soup bowl.

MENU A-2　炸核桃鶏片

DEEP-FRIED WALNUT CHICKEN

Ingredients:

½ lb. (250 g) chicken breasts
2 egg whites
4 tablespoons cornstarch
2 cups walnuts, chopped
Canned pineapple ⎫
Maraschino cherry ⎬ for garnish
Green pepper ⎭
Mixture (a):
⎧ 1½ teaspoons salt
⎨ Pepper
⎩ 2 teaspoons rice wine
4 cups oil for frying

Methods:

1.   Cut chicken breasts into bite size and mix with mixture (a).

2.   Beat egg white lightly, add cornstarch and mix well.

3.   Dip chicken into egg-white mixture and coat with walnuts.

4.   Heat oil to 375° F (190°C). Drop the walnut-coated chicken pieces, one by one, into pan and deep-fry until light brown. Remove from oil and drain. Place on a serving plate and garnish with pineapple, cherry and green pepper arranged like a butterfly (see photo).

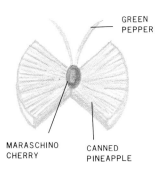

GREEN PEPPER

MARASCHINO CHERRY

CANNED PINEAPPLE

1

2–3

3

4

OVER MEDIUM HEAT

MENU A-3　咕咾肉

SWEET-SOUR PORK

Ingredients:
1 lb. (500 g) lean boneless pork
Seasoning:

(a) ⎰ 1 teaspoon rice wine
⎱ ½ teaspoon salt
¼ teaspoon pepper

Coating:

(b) ⎰ 1 egg
⎱ 1 tablespoon flour
1 tablespoon cornstarch

5 cups oil for deep-frying
½ of a carrot, peeled and par-
    boiled, cut in bite size
3 dried mushrooms, soaked and
    quartered
3 cups onion, cut in bite size
⅔ cup cucumber, cut in bite size
1 clove garlic, peeled and sliced
Mixture:

(c) ⎰ 4 tablespoons tomato
        ketchup
    1 teaspoon soy sauce
    4 tablespoons vinegar
    4 tablespoons sugar
    ¾ cup water
    1½ tablespoons cornstarch

Method:

1. Cut meat into bite size.

2. Sprinkle it with rice seasoning (a) on all sides.

3. Mix (b) in a bowl and dip pork into it. Heat frying oil to 375°F (190°C). Deep-fry pork pieces one by one until light brown. Remove from oil and drain.

4. Sauté vegetables all at once in same pan for 1 minute. Remove from pan and drain.

5. Mix (c) well together. Heat 5 tablespoons oil in another pan, add (c) mixture and cook until thick.

6. Return pork and vegetables into sauce and mix well.

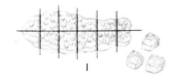

OVER MEDIUM HEAT

凉拍黄瓜

CUCUM-BER SALAD

Ingredients:

6 radishes
1 cucumber (about ¾ lb., 400 g)
½ carrot, shredded
1 teaspoon salt
1 tablespoon salad oil
2 teaspoons sugar
3 tablespoons vinegar
3 tablespoons soy sauce

Method:

1. Prepare radish flowers as illustrated. Soak in ice water with ½ teaspoon salt for 20 minutes.

2. Cut cucumber and remove seeds. Pound lightly with flat of heavy knife or cleaver.

3. Cut cucumber into 1 or 2-inch (3～5 cm) lengths.

4. Mix ½ teaspoon salt, salad oil, sugar, vinegar and soy sauce well.

5. Pour (4) over cucumber. Garnish with carrot and radish.

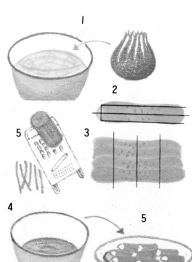

MENU A-5

蛋炒飯

EGG FRIED RICE

Ingredients:
7 eggs
5 cups cold cooked white rice
  (see page 21)
3 slices ham, chopped
3 tablespoons green peas
⅓ cup scallion, shredded
3 tablespoons oil
¾ teaspoon salt

Method:
1. Beat eggs in a bowl, adding a pinch of salt.

2. Heat oil, add eggs and cook for 1 minute over medium heat.

3. Add rice and fry well, mixing with eggs.

4. Add ham, green peas, scallion and salt mixing well until heated through.

MENU B

1. Vegetable Soup
2. Beef with Snow Peas
3. Deep-Fried Pork
4. Fresh Ginger Oysters
5. Boiled Rice

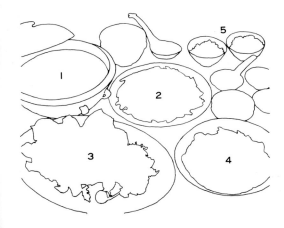

MENU B-1 素菜湯

VEGETABLE SOUP

Ingredients:
2 tomatoes (about 8 oz., 240 g)
6 cups chicken stock
3–4 cabbage leaves, shredded
½ carrot, thinly sliced
½ onion, thinly sliced
½ stalk celery, thinly sliced
3 tablespoons oil
1 tablespoon salt
¼ teaspoon pepper
1 teaspoon seasame or salad oil
½ teaspoon Tabasco (optional)

Method:
1.   Blanch tomato for half a minute and peel off skin. Remove seeds and cut into small pieces.

2.   Add cabbage, carrot, onion and celery to boiling chicken stock and bring to boil again. Reduce heat and cook until tender.

3.   Sauté tomato in 3 tablespoons oil. Add to soup with salt and pepper. Cook for another 3 or 4 minutes and add sesame oil and Tabasco.

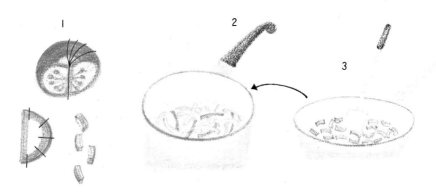

MENU B-2 雪豆牛肉

BEEF WITH SNOW PEAS

Ingredients:

12 oz. (350 g) beef fillet

Marinade:

(a) {
⅓ teaspoon baking soda
¾ teaspoon sugar
½ teaspoon salt
1½ teaspoons cornstarch
1½ tablespoons soy sauce
2 tablespoons water
}

2 tablespoons salad oil

½ lb (250 g) snow peas, strung

1 teaspoon fresh ginger of ¼ teaspoon ginger powder

4-inch (10 cm) long scallion

4 cups oil for deep-frying

Mixture:

(b) {
1 teaspoon cornstarch
1 tablespoon water
1 tablespoon sesame or salad oil
}

½ teaspoon salt

Method:

1. Cut beef in bite-size slices, marinate in (a) for 30 minutes, then add 2 tablespoons oil and mix well.

2. Heat frying oil to 320°F (160°C) and deep-fry beef for 1 minute. Drain. Pound fresh ginger and scallion lightly.

3. Leave 2 tablespoons oil in pan, fry ginger and scallion and stir in beef and mix well for 1 minute. Add (b) mixture, and cook until thick. Remove fresh ginger and scallion. Remove to hot serving plate.

4. Heat 2 tablespoons oil, add ½ teaspoon salt and cook snow peas for 2 minutes. Arrange on serving plate as garnish.

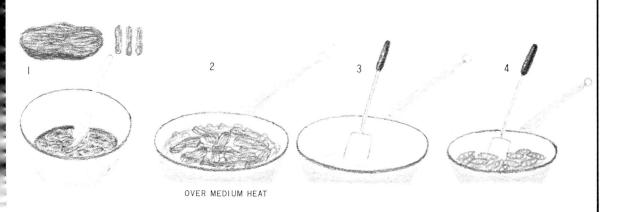

1   2   3   4

OVER MEDIUM HEAT

MENU B-3 油炸肉

DEEP FRIED PORK

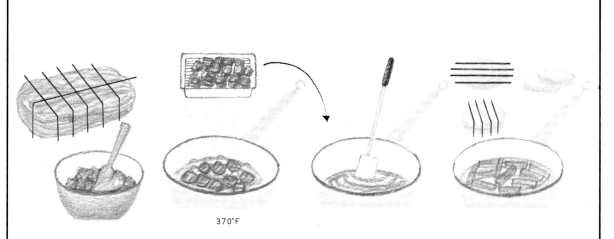

370°F

Ingredients:
1¼ lb. (600 g) pork brisket or pork
   chop
4-inch (10 cm) long scallion
Marinade:
(a) { 1½ tablespoons rice wine
      4 tablespoons soy sauce
      ¼ teaspoon ginger powder
4 cups oil for frying
1 tablespoon sugar
3 potatoes
Leaf lettuce

Method:
1. Cut pork into 1-inch (2.5 cm) by 2-inch (5 cm) pieces. With flat of knife pound scallion lightly. Marinate pork in marinade (a) and scallion for 30 minutes.

2. Heat oil and deep-fry pork until brown. Remove from oil and drain.

3. Heat marinade. Add sugar, cook for a few seconds, return fried pork to sauce and stir well. Remove to plate.

4. Peel potatoes and cut into finger size strips. Soak in cold water and drain. Deep-fry in oil until light brown.

5. Remove to serving plate and garnish with leaf lettuce.

MENU B-4 薑蔥生蠔

FRESH GINGER OYSTER

Ingredients:

30 oysters, shucked
8-inch (20 cm) scallion long, cut in
  ½-inch (1 cm) lengths
2 oz. (50 g) fresh ginger, peeled and
  sliced
2 cloves garlic, sliced
5 tablespoons oil
Seasoning:
  4 tablespoons rice wine
  4 tablespoons soy sauce
  ⅓ teaspoon salt
  ½ tablespoon sugar
5 tablespoons oil

Methods:

1. Put oysters in boiling water and cook for 30 seconds. Wash and drain well.

2. Heat oil. Add scallion, ginger and garlic and fry for a few seconds. Add oyster and seasoning all at once. Stir quickly over high heat.

MENU B-5

白 飯 　　 BOILED RICE

Ingredients:

3 cups rice
3½ cups water

Method:

1. Wash rice in large bowl with cold water by rubbing gently between thumb and fingers. Drain and repeat this procedure 5 or 6 times until water is clear. Drain well and set aside for 30 minutes.

2. Put drained rice and water in covered pan and cook over high heat. When it comes to boil, reduce the heat to low and cook for 10 minutes more. Turn flame on high again and remove from heat.

3. Let stand, covered, for about 10 minutes before serving.

MENU C

1. Chicken Noodle Soup
2. Vegetable Toast
3. Creamed Chinese Cabbage
4. Shredded Beef with Green Pepper & Onion
5. Steamed Chinese Cakes

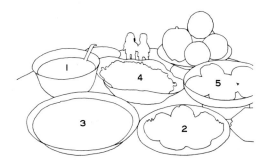

MENU C-1 鷄湯麵

CHICKEN NOODLE SOUP

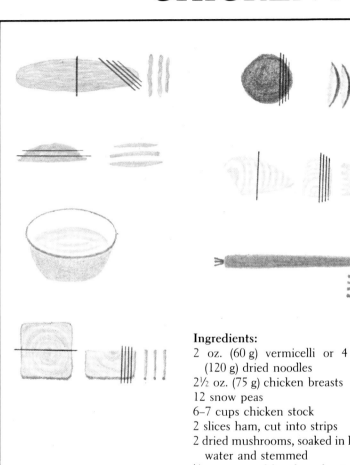

Ingredients:

2 oz. (60 g) vermicelli or 4 oz. (120 g) dried noodles
2½ oz. (75 g) chicken breasts
12 snow peas
6–7 cups chicken stock
2 slices ham, cut into strips
2 dried mushrooms, soaked in hot water and stemmed
⅓ cup canned bamboo shoots
1 carrot
1 tablespoon salt
Dash of pepper

Methods:

1. Drop vermicelli into boiling water and boil for 5 minutes. Drain, rinse and drain again. Set aside.

2. Slice chicken meat and snow peas into thin strips.

3. Shred ham, mushroom, bamboo shoots and carrot.

4. Bring chicken stock to boiling point. Add chicken meat, ham, snow peas, mushroom, bamboo shoots and carrot. Cook for 2 minutes. Add salt and pepper to taste. Add cooked vermicelli and boil for 1 minute over medium heat.

MENU C-2 素炸吐司

VEGETABLE TOAST

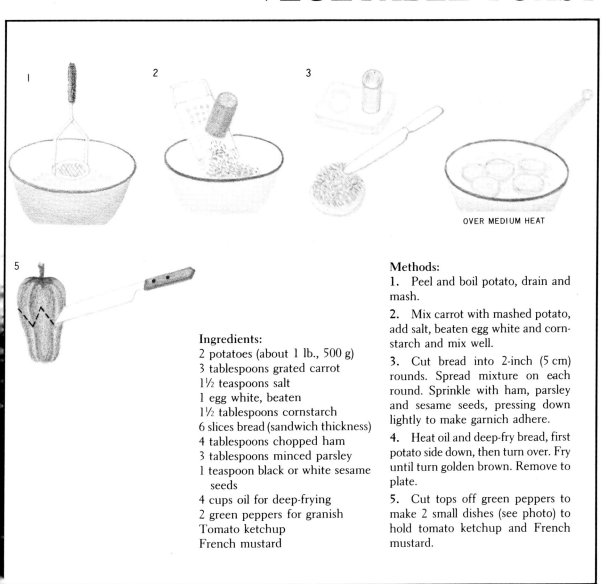

OVER MEDIUM HEAT

Ingredients:
2 potatoes (about 1 lb., 500 g)
3 tablespoons grated carrot
1½ teaspoons salt
1 egg white, beaten
1½ tablespoons cornstarch
6 slices bread (sandwich thickness)
4 tablespoons chopped ham
3 tablespoons minced parsley
1 teaspoon black or white sesame
    seeds
4 cups oil for deep-frying
2 green peppers for granish
Tomato ketchup
French mustard

Methods:
1.   Peel and boil potato, drain and mash.

2.   Mix carrot with mashed potato, add salt, beaten egg white and cornstarch and mix well.

3.   Cut bread into 2-inch (5 cm) rounds. Spread mixture on each round. Sprinkle with ham, parsley and sesame seeds, pressing down lightly to make garnich adhere.

4.   Heat oil and deep-fry bread, first potato side down, then turn over. Fry until turn golden brown. Remove to plate.

5.   Cut tops off green peppers to make 2 small dishes (see photo) to hold tomato ketchup and French mustard.

MENU C-3 奶油白菜

CREAMED CHINESE CABBAGE

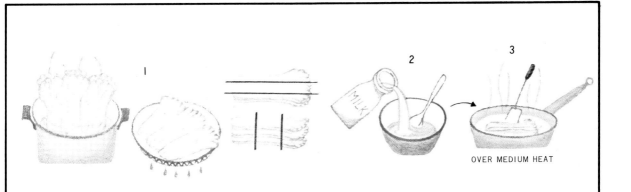

1

2

3

OVER MEDIUM HEAT

Ingredients:
1 small Chinese cabbage (about
  2 lb., 1 kg)
1 teaspoon salt
Mixture:
(a) { 2 cups milk
     1½ tablespoons cornstarch
     ¾ teaspoon salt
6 tablespoons oil
1 hard-boiled egg yolk, minced
Parsley, minced
1 teaspoon paprika

Method:
1. Parboil Chinese cabbage in water with 1 teaspoon salt until tender and drain. Then cut it into 3 or 4-inch (7.5 or 10 cm) lengths.

2. Mix (a) well together, and set aside.

3. Heat oil, add cabbage and sauté for 2 minutes. Add milk mixture and stir well until thickened. Remove to warmed plate and sprinkle with egg yolk, parsley and paprika.

MENU C-4

青椒牛肉絲

SHRED-DED BEEF WITH GREEN PEPPER AND ONION

Ingredients:
1 lb. (500 g) beef rump steak, shredded

Marinade:

(a)
- 2 teaspoons oil
- 1 tablespoon rice wine
- 1 teaspoon cornstarch
- ¼ teaspoon baking soda
- 1 tablespoon soy sauce
- ½ teaspoon sugar

6 tablespoons oil
¾ teaspoon salt
2 onions, shredded
2 green peppers, shredded
Pinch of pepper

Methods:

1. Sprinkle beef with (a). Set aside for 30 minutes.

2. Heat 3 tablespoons oil in pan; add ¾ teaspoon salt. Stir in onions and fry for 2 minutes. Add green peppers; fry for 2 minutes. Remove from pan.

3. Heat 3 more tablespoons oil in same pan. Add beef. Stir until color changes. Add a pinch of pepper and vegetables. Mix well for 1 minute.

OVER MEDIUM HEAT

清蒸蛋糕

STEAM-ED CHINESE CAKES

Ingredients:
6 eggs
6 tablespoons sugar
6 tablespoons flour
Few drops of almond extract
2 tablespoons raisins
6 each candied red and green
   cherries or other candied fruit
Lard or shortening

Method:
1. Beat egg and sugar hard with wire whisk or mixer.

2. Add flour and a few drops of almond extract and mix well, but gently.

3. Chop candied fruit. Grease 6 pyrex cups with lard or shortening. Sprinkle fruit on bottom of cups. Pour batter over this.

4. Steam for 20 minutes. Remove gently and set on warmed plate.

OVER MEDIUM HEAT

MENU D

1. Sour & Hot Soup
2. Braised Pork
   with Chestnuts
3. Egg Sandwich Chinese
4. Sweet & Sour Prawns
5. Glazed Apples

MENU D-1 酸辣湯

SOUR AND HOT SOUP

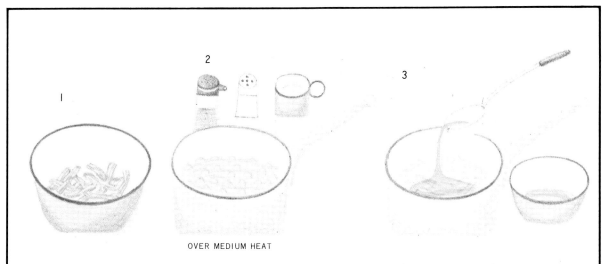

OVER MEDIUM HEAT

Ingredients:
2 oz. (60 g) boneless pork, shredded
Pinch of salt
Pepper
1 teaspoon cornstarch
5 cups chicken stock
½ carrot, parboiled
2 ~ 3 dried mushrooms, soaked
   in warm water and stemmed
⅓ cup canned bamboo shoots
4 ~ 5 slices ham
3 eggs, beaten
Mixture:
⎧ 2 tablespoons soy sauce
⎪ 2 tablespoons vinegar
(a) ⎨ 5 teaspoons cornstarch
⎪ 1½ teaspoons salt
⎩ 4½ tablespoons water
½ teaspoon pepper

Method:
1. Dredge pork with pinch of salt and pepper and 1 teaspoon cornstarch.

2. Shred carrot, mushrooms, bamboo shoots and ham.

3. Bring chicken stock to boil. Add salt, pork, carrot, mushroom, bamboo shoots and ham, cooking for 2 minutes. Add mixture (a). Stir for a few seconds until soup thickens.

4. Slowly pour in beaten eggs in a fine thread, stirring gently. Add pepper for taste.*

*   If you prefer hot seasoning, you may add a few drops of Tabasco.

MENU D-2

栗子紅燒肉

BRAISED PORK WITH CHEST-NUTS

OVER MEDIUM HEAT

Ingredients:
2 lb. (1 kg) pork shoulder or fresh ham
¼ scallion, thinly sliced on diagonal
1 teaspoon chopped, fresh ginger, or ¼ teaspoon ginger powder
18 canned or fresh* chestnuts
6 tablespoons oil
2 tablespoons rice wine
6 tablespoons soy sauce
1½ cups water
3 tablespoons rock candy or crystalized sugar

Method:
1. Cut pork into 1-inch (3 cm) cubes.

2. Heat 4 tablespoons oil. Add scallion, ginger and pork cubes. Stir until pork changes color. Add rice wine, soy sauce and water; bring to boil. Cover pan and reduce heat to low. Simmer for 30 minutes.

3. Add canned chestnuts and rock candy. Cook for another 15 minutes.

* If fresh chestnuts are used, boil and peel off shells and inner brown membranes, add rock candy and cook for 30 minutes.

荷包蛋

EGG SAND-WICH CHINESE

Ingredients:
6 eggs
3 teaspoons oil
2 tablespoons soy sauce
1 teaspoon sugar
1 tablespoon water
6 butter rolls/Lettuce leaves

Method:
1. Break one egg into small bowl.

2. Heat ½ teaspoon oil and fry each egg separately. When egg has set, fold over in half-moon shape. Remove to plate.

3. Add soy sauce, sugar, water to same pan, bring to boil, add eggs and cook for 1½ minutes.

4. Put fried egg and lettuce leaf between split rolls (see photo).

OVER MEDIUM HEAT

MENU D-4 裹大蝦

SWEET AND SOUR PRAWNS

Ingredients:
12 prawns
1 cucumber, sliced
Seasoning:

(a)
- 3 tablespoons soy sauce
- 3 tablespoons vinegar
- 1½ tablespoons rice wine
- 1½ tablespoons sugar
- ⅓ teaspoon salt
- 3 teaspoons cornstarch

1 teaspoon cornstarch
4 cups oil for deep-frying
3 tablespoons oil
Salt and pepper

Method:

1. Wash prawns and remove shell except at tail. Remove black veins and slice along back, without cutting through, as shown in illustration. Sprinkle a dash of salt and pepper and coat with cornstarch.

2. Mix seasoning (a) in a bowl.

3. Heat frying oil to 375°F (190°C). Add prawns, deep-fry for 1 minute, remove from oil and drain.

4. Heat 3 tablespoons oil in pan, cook (a) mixture until thick. Place prawns into mixture and mix well. Garnish with cucumber.

MENU D-5 拔絲薛菓

GLAZED APPLES

Ingredients:
3 medium-sized apples
Batter:
    2 egg whites
    4 tablespoons all-purpose flour
    2 teaspoons cornstarch
Syrup:
    2 tablespoons water
    1⅓ cups sugar
    1 tablespoon oil
1 teaspoon black or white sesame
    seeds
⅓ teaspoon salt
4 cups oil for deep-frying

Method:

1.   Cut apple into 8 wedges; peel and core. Place in water with salt added.

2.   Beat egg white and mix with flour and cornstarch until smooth.

3.   Drain apples and coat with batter.

4.   Heat oil to 375°F (190°C). Deep-fry apples until light amber, remove from oil and drain.

5.   Bring water and sugar to boil over high heat, stirring, only until sugar dissolves. Add 1 tablespoon oil, stir constantly until syrup instantly forms hard mass in iced water. Put fried apples and black or white sesame seeds into syrup.*

6.   Remove well-coated glazed apples to lightly greased serving plate. Dip each piece quickly into bowl of ice water before eating.

*   Syrup should form threads as you remove the apples (see photo).

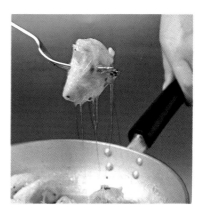

MENU E

1. Won Ton Soup
2. Eggplant with
   Meat & Garlic
3. Shrimp in Hot Sauce
4. Deep-Fried Chicken
5. Hot Orange Juice

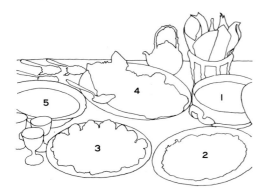

MENU E-1 餛飩湯

WON TON SOUP

Ingredients:

For won ton skin:
1 egg
6½ tablespoons water
3 cups flour

For filling:
1 cup spinach leaves,
    boiled and chopped
¾ cup minced pork
1 tablespoon minced
    scallion (optional)
½ teaspoon salt
½ teaspoon sugar
¼ teaspoon pepper
2 teaspoons rice wine
6 cups chicken stock
12 snow peas, boiled
Egg sheet*, cut into strips
Salt and pepper

Method:

To make won ton skin:

1. In bowl beat egg and mix with water. Add flour and mix well.

2. Knead for about 1 minute into stiff dough. Cover with damp cloth and set aside for about 30 minutes.

3. Roll out dough about ¹⁄₁₆ inch (2 mm) thick. Cut out 20 squares, 3 inches (7½ cm) by 3 inches (7½ cm), for won ton skins.

To make won ton:

1. Mix spinach, pork, scallion, salt, sugar, pepper, and rice wine well.

2. Place ½ teaspoon of meat mixture in center of each skin. Bring opposite corners together in fold. Seal by dotting bottom edge with water and pinching together firmly. Fold other two corners toward each other. See illustration.

3. Cook won ton in boiling water for 3 minutes and remove to 6 individual bowls.

4. Bring chicken stock to boil, add a pinch of salt and pepper and pour broth over won ton.

5. Garnish with snow peas, egg sheet and serve immediately.

* To make egg sheet:

1. Beat one egg with a pinch of salt and sherry.

2. Heat 1 teaspoon oil in frying pan over medium heat, cooking pan evenly.

3. Pour in egg rotating quickly to cover bottom of pan.

4. Cook until lightly browned. Remove to cutting board and cut into strips.

MENU E-2　魚香茄子

EGGPLANT WITH MEAT AND GARLIC

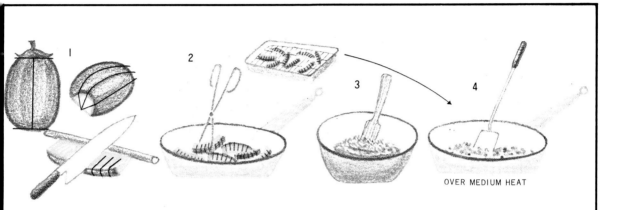

OVER MEDIUM HEAT

Ingredients:
2 large-sized eggplants
5 oz. (150 g) ground pork
3 tablespoons soaked and chopped
   Chinese mushrooms
2 teaspoons minced garlic
Seasoning:

(a) { 2½ tablespoons soy sauce
     1½ tablespoons rice wine
     ½ teaspoon cornstarch

Pepper
1 teaspoon salt
1 teaspoon sugar
1 teaspoon salad or sesame oil
4 cups oil for deep-frying

Method:
1. Remove stems from eggplants. Cut each into 12 lengthwise pieces and cut gashes in each piece (as shown).

2. Heat frying oil to 375°F (190°C), deep-fry eggplant for 2 minutes.

3. Mix seasoning (a) with ground pork, mushroom and garlic.

4. Heat 3 tablespoons oil in pan, sauté pork mixture for 2 minutes. Add fried eggplant and mix well. Add a dash of pepper, salt and sugar and stir well. Quickly stir in salad or sesame oil.

MENU E-3 干燒蝦仁

SHRIMP IN HOT SAUCE

OVER MEDIUM HEAT

Ingredients:
2½ cups (1 lb., 500 g) shelled
  shrimp
1½ tablespoons minced fresh
  ginger
1 tablespoon minced garlic
6 tablespoon chopped scallion
1 broccoli (10 oz., 300 g)
Coating:
(a) { 1 tablespoon sherry
    ½ egg white
    1 teaspoon cornstarch
Seasoning:
(b) { 2 teaspoons Tabasco
    4½ tablespoons tomato
      ketchup
    1 tablespoon soy sauce
    1 tablespoon sugar
    1½ teaspoons vinegar
    ½ teaspoon salt
⅓ cup chicken stock or water
2 tablespoons cornstarch dissolved
  in 3 or 4 tablespoons water
2 cups oil for sautéing

Method:
1. Remove black vein from shrimp,
wash in salted water and drain. Mix
with (a).

2. Divide clusters of flower buds of
broccoli and boil in salted water. Arrange on serving plate as garnish.

3. In oil heated to 350°F (175°C),
sauté shrimp, stirring briskly. Do not
overcook. Remove from oil and drain.

4. Leave 4 tablespoons heated oil in
pan. Sauté ginger, garlic and scallion
for 1 minute. Add (b) and shrimp.
Pour in chicken stock or water, cook
for 2 minutes, stirring constantly.
Thicken with dissolved cornstarch.
Remove to serving plate.

炸子鷄

DEEP FRIED CHICK-EN

Ingredients:
12 chicken drumsticks
½ cup shredded scallion
Marinade:

(a) { 4 tablespoons soy sauce
2 tablespoons rice wine
¼ teaspoon pepper

⅓ cup cornstarch and
⅓ cup flower, mixed
4 cups oil for deep-frying

Method:
1. Marinate chicken drumsticks in (a) for 30 minutes.

2. Coat each chicken drumsticks with cornstarch mixture. Heat oil to 375°F (190°C), deep-fry chicken drumsticks until golden brown and drain.

3. Drain pan, put in scallions and fried chicken drumsticks, stirring over heat for 1 minute so scallions stick to chicken. If desired, garnish plate with flower made from giant radish, as shown in photo.

OVER MEDIUM HEAT

MENU E-5

橙子羹

HOT
ORANGE
JUICE

Ingredients:
4 cups water
1½ cups (11 oz., 325 g) sugar
3 oranges, squeezed
3 oranges, sectioned
3 tablespoons cornstarch dissolved
  in 3 tablespoons water
3 maraschino cherries
Angelica, sliced

Method:
1. Combine water and sugar in saucepan; bring to boil over high heat. Add orange juice and sections, stirring until sugar is dissolved. Add dissolved cornstarch, stirring constantly until thickened.

2. Pour into serving bowl garnished with sliced cherries and angelica as shown in photo.

MENU F

1. Tomato Egg Soup
2. Sweet & Sour Cabbage
3. Braised Duck in Wine
4. Shrimp Chow-Mein
5. Almond Jelly

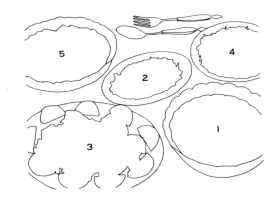

62

蕃茄蛋花湯

TOMATO EGG SOUP

Ingredients:
2 tomatoes
5 cups chicken stock
1 egg, beaten
Few sprigs of spinach
1½ teaspoons salt
1 teaspoon salad or sesame oil

Method:

1. Cut tomato into thin wedges, removing seeds.

2. Bring tomato and chicken stock to boil. Add salt to taste.

3. Pour beaten egg in fine thread and bring to boil. Add spinach and again bring to boil. Remove from heat and sprinkle with salad or sesame oil.

MENU F-2

糖醋卷心菜

SWEET AND SOUR CAB-BAGE

Ingredients:
3 lb (1.5 kg) cabbage, shredded
1½ tablespoons salt
2 ~ 3 green peppers, shredded
2 fresh red peppers or pimentos, shredded
4½ tablespoons vinegar
4½ tablespoons sugar
6 tablespoons oil

Method:
1. Heat 3 tablespoons oil in pan, add salt first, then peppers. Stir for 1 minute and remove to plate.

2. Heat 3 tablespoons oil in same pan, add cabbage, cook for 2 minutes. Add peppers and mix well.

3. Mix together vinegar and sugar and add to pan; cook, tossing well for 2 or 3 minutes. Serve hot or cold.

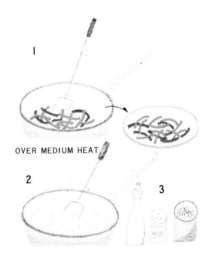

MENU F-3 酒燜鴨

BRAISED DUCK IN WINE

Ingredients:

1 duck (about 4½ lb., 12 kg), cut in serving pieces
¼ leek
1 orange
1 cup rice wine
⅓ cup water
6 tablespoons soy sauce
2 tablespoons rock candy or crystalized sugar

Method:

1. Put duck into Dutch oven with leek and rice wine and bring to boil.

2. Slice orange. Add half of it to pan. Add water, soy sauce and rock candy.

3. Cover and reduce heat to low and cook for 20 minutes.

4. Transfer to 375°F (190°C) oven, braise for 1 hour. Remove to hot plate. Garnish with orange slices.

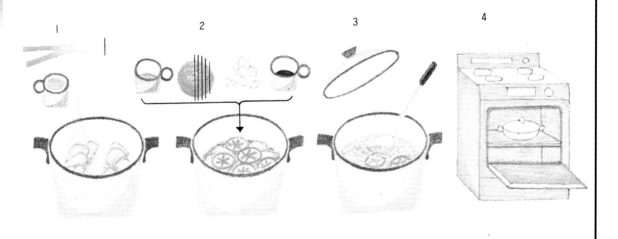

MENU F-4 蝦仁炒麺

SHRIMP CHOW-MEIN

Ingredient:
¾ lb. (325 g) thin
   spaghetti (Chinese
   noodles if available)
5 oz. (150 g) shelled shrimp
   (frozen)
2 cups water
½ bunch spinach
1⅔ teaspoons salt
Pepper
5 teaspoons rice wine
4½ tablespoons oil

Method:
1. Cook spaghetti in boiling water and drain.

2. Wash shrimp first in 2 cups of water with 1 teaspoon salt added, then rinse with cold water and drain. Sprinkle with a dash of pepper and 2 teaspoons rice wine.

3. Cut spinach into 2 (5 cm) or 3-inch (8 cm) lengths. Wash and drain.

4. Heat 1½ tablespoons oil in pan, sauté shrimp, add ⅓ teaspoon salt, stir for 1 minute over high heat and remove from pan.

5. Heat 1½ tablespoons oil in same pan, add ⅓ teaspoon salt first, then spinach. Toss quickly for half a minute over high heat and remove from pan.

6. Heat 1½ tablespoons oil in same pan. Add spaghetti, shrimp, spinach and 3 teaspoons rice wine and stir well. Add a pinch of salt to taste.

MENU F-5 杏仁豆腐

ALMOND JELLY

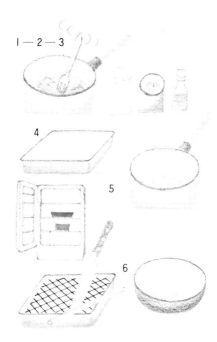

Ingredients:

2 packages unflavoured gelatin
  (about 2 tablespoons)
1 cup plus 2 tablespoons water
1 cup milk
¾ cup sugar
½ teaspoon almond extract
Syrup:
  1 cup sugar
  4 cups water
6 slices pineapple
6 cherries

Method:

1. Sprinkle gelatin on 2 tablespoons water to soften.

2. Bring 1 cup of water to boil. Add gelatin and stir until dissolved.

3. Stir in milk, sugar and ¼ teaspoon almond extract.

4. Pour mixture into flat pan. Cool in refrigerator.

5. Bring sugar and water to boil to make syrup. When cool, add ¼ teaspoon almond extract and chill in refrigerator.

6. Cut almond jelly into diamond shapes and pour syrup over it. Pour into serving bowl and garnish with pineapple and cherry as shown in photograph.

DINNERS FOR SMALL ENTERTAINMENTS

New Year's Day Dinner
Chinese Pancake Dinner
Chinese Fondue Dinner
Valentine's Day Dinner
Halloween Dinner

I
New Year's Day Dinner

(Serves 4 to 6)

Menu
(1) Assorted Appetizers
(2) Abalone Soup
(3) Stir-Fried Lobster Meat
(4) Stuffed Duck

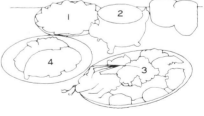

(1)
Assorted
Appetizers

什錦冷盆

Ingredients:
1. Cheese
2. Smoked beef
3. Cucumbers
4. Barbecued pork
5. Abalone (canned)
6. Roast duck
7. Braised mushrooms
8. Ham
9. Steamed chicken breast
10. { Sliced tomatoes
     Asparagus
     Cherries
     Parsley }
Dip: Soy sauce
     Vinegar
     Dry mustard

Method:
1. Slice ingredients 1 to 9 into small pieces.

2. Arrange all ingredients as shown in photo. If some ingredients are not available, substitute any other ingredient on hand.

3. Dip into mixture of soy sauce, vinegar, and mustard to eat.

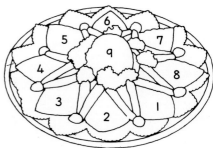

(2)
Abalone
Soup

鮑片湯

Ingredients:
5 cups chicken stock
1 small piece fresh ginger, peeled
1 scallion
½ cup sliced carrot
½ cup sliced celery
½ cup sliced canned abalone
1½ teaspoons salt

Method:
1.   Bring stock to boil, add ginger, scallion, carrot, and celery. Cook for 15 minutes.

2.   Add abalone and boil gently for 1 minute. Add salt to taste. Remove ginger and scallion and pour soup into heated tureen.

NEW YEAR'S DINNER

(3) Stir-Fried Lobster Meat 炒龍蝦片

Ingredients:
1 live lobster (2–2½ lb., 1–1.1 kg)
12 raw prawns or jumbo shrimps
4 tablespoons oil
Salt
2 lb. (1 kg) frozen or fresh spinach
{ 2 tablespoons rice wine
  2 teaspoons cornstarch
  1 egg white
½ cup sliced onion
½ cup sliced carrot
½ teaspoon salt
3 cups for deep-frying oil
Tomato, pineapple rings,
    cucumber and cherries for
    garnish

Method:
1.   Cut lobster into 3 parts. Twist off claws. Remove meat from shell. Slice meat.

2.   Shell prawns, remove black veins and slice.

3.   Steam head and tail shells of lobster about 20 minutes.

4.   Heat 2 tablespoons oil in pan. Add a dash of salt and fry spinach for 2 minutes. Remove to large plate. Arrange steamed lobster head and tail shells on spinach.

5.   Mix meat of lobster and prawn together with wine, cornstarch and egg white.

6.   Heat 3 cups of frying oil to 350°F (175°C). Pour lobster mixture into oil, stir for 2 minutes until color changes. Remove from pan and drain.

7.   Heat 2 tablespoons of the same oil in pan, add onion and carrot. Stir for 2 minutes. Add lobster mixture and salt, mix well. Remove to the middle of plate of spinach as shown in photograph. Garnish with slices of tomato, pineapple rings, cucumber slices and cherries as shown in photo.

NEW YEAR'S DINNER

(4) Stuffed Duck 八寶鴨

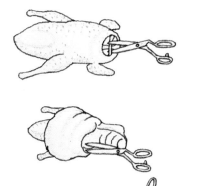

Ingredients:
4–5 lb. (1.8–2.2 kg) whole duck
Salt and pepper
4 cups cooked glutinous rice*
½ cup very finely diced
    lean pork
1 duck liver (diced)
3 dried mushrooms
    (soaked and diced)
1 bamboo shoot (diced)
2 tablespoons rice wine
2 tablespoons soy sauce
1 teaspoon sugar
2 cups water
5 tablespoons soy sauce
1 scallion and 1 small piece
    fresh ginger, peeled
2 tablespoons sugar
5 cups oil for deep-frying

* Soak rice for 30 minutes before cooking. Cook rice in cold water over high heat until boiling. Turn heat to low. Cook 20 minutes.

Method:
1. Bone duck as illustrated. Wash outside with hot water and wipe inside with paper towel. Season with salt and pepper.

2. Mix cooked glutinous rice* with diced pork, liver, mushrooms, bamboo shoot and 1 tablespoon rice wine, 2 tablespoons soy sauce, 1 teaspoon sugar and a dash of salt and pepper.

3. Stuff rice mixture into the cavity of duck and close up opening with clips or trussing pins. Rub duck skin with soy sauce.

4. Heat frying oil to 375°F (190°C) in a large deep fat fryer. Deep-fry duck until golden brown. Remove and drain.

5. Place fried duck in 2 cups of water. Add remaining 1 tablespoon rice wine, 5 tablespoons soy sauce, fresh ginger and scallion. Cook; uncovered, over low heat for ¾ hour. Add sugar and cook another 15 minutes.

6. Cut duck into two or more pieces. Serve hot. Eat duck and rice together.

II
Chinese
Pancake
Dinner

(Serves 6)

Menu
(1) Pancakes
(2) Chop Suey
(3) Chicken with
    Green Pepper
(4) Egg with Shrimp
(5) Fried Shredded
    Potato
(6) Chicken Soup

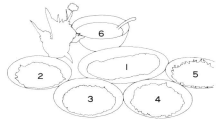

(1) Pancakes 薄 餅

Ingredients:
2 cups sifted flour
¾ cup boiling water
2 tablespoons lard, vegetable
  shortening, sesame oil or
  salad oil

Method:

1. Mix flour with boiling water. Knead well on unfloured board into soft dough. Cover and set aside for 15 minutes.

2. Roll dough into a sausage shape about 1½ inches (3.5 cm) in diameter.

3. Cut dough into 12 pieces. Flatten each piece with the palm. Brush salad oil lightly on one side of each piece. Place two pieces together with oiled side inside like a sandwich.

4. Roll out each sandwich into a 6- to 7-inch (15 to 17.5 cm) circle.

5. Bake in flat, ungreased frying pan over low heat for 1 minute and turn over. Bake the other side until slightly browned.

6. Remove from heat and separate each sandwich into two thin pancakes. To re-heat, steam for 10 minutes or wrap in wet cloth and place in microwave range for half a minute. Serve with other dishes.

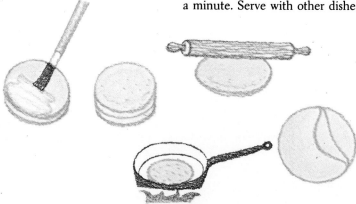

(2) Chop Suey 炒和菜

Ingredients:

3 cups bean sprouts, canned or fresh

Seasoning:

(a) {
1 teaspoon rice wine
½ tablespoon soy sauce
½ teaspoon cornstarch
¼ teaspoon pepper
}

1 cup shredded lean pork

1 cup shredded onion

2 cups shredded cabbage
½ cup shredded bamboo shoots
½ cup shredded carrot
½ cup shredded mushrooms
12 snow peas (strung and shredded)

Seasoning:

(b) {
1 teaspoon salt
1 teaspoon sugar
1 tablespoon soy sauce
}

6 tablespoons salad oil

Method:

1. Clean bean sprouts.

2. Mix (a) with shredded pork. Heat 3 tablespoons oil and sauté pork until it changes color. Remove to plate.

3. Heat 3 tablespoons oil in the same pan and sauté onion, cabbage, bamboo shoots, carrots, mushrooms, snow peas and bean sprouts for 3 minutes.

4. Add (b) seasoning and stir for 1 minute. Mix in pork. Remove to heated plate and serve hot.

(3) Chicken with Green Pepper 青椒鷄絲

Ingredients:

1½ cups shredded chicken breast

Seasoning:

(a) {
⅓ teaspoon salt
¼ teaspoon pepper
1 tablespoon rice wine
1 tablespoon cornstarch
1 egg white
}

½ cup shredded scallions or leeks

1½ cups shredded bamboo shoots
1 cup shredded green pepper

Seasoning:

(b) {
1 teaspoon salt
½ teaspoon sugar
½ tablespoon vinegar
}

½ cup shredded ham
2 cups vegetable oil
4 tablespoons salad oil

Method:

1. Mix shredded chicken with (a).

2. To heated pan, add 2 cups of oil and heat to 350°F (175°C). Stir in chicken and cook until it changes color. Remove and drain.

3. Heat 4 tablespoons oil in pan. Sauté shredded scallions, bamboo shoots, and green peppers for 2 minutes. Add chicken and (b) seasoning. Mix well.

4. Remove to hot serving plate and granish with shredded ham.

(4) Egg with Shrimp 蝦仁炒蛋

Ingredients:
4 eggs
Seasoning:
(a) { ⅓ teaspoon salt
{ 1 teaspoon rice wine
1 cup shelled and
  deveined raw shrimp
(b) { ¼ teaspoon salt
{ ¼ teaspoon pepper
{ 1 teaspoon rice wine
{ 1 teaspoon cornstarch
4 tablespoons salad oil

Method:
1.   Beat eggs with (a) seasoning.
2.   Wash shrimp, drain, and mix with (b) ingredients.
3.   Heat 4 tablespoons oil in pan and sauté shrimp over medium heat for 1 minute. Add egg mixture to shrimp and fry until set.
4.   Remove to heated plate and serve hot.

(6) Chicken Soup 鷄塊湯

Ingredients:
2 chicken legs
6 dried Chinese mushrooms
1 small bamboo shoot
6 cups water
1 scallion
1 small piece ginger, peeled
1 tablespoon rice wine
1½ teaspoons salt

Method:
1.   Wash chicken legs in running hot water and cut into bite-size pieces.
2.   Soak Chinese mushrooms in ½ cup warm water for 10 minutes and remove stems.
3.   Cut bamboo shoot into bite-size pieces.
4.   Cook chicken in 6 cups of water over high heat. Add scallion, ginger and wine. Bring water to boil, skimming off any scum or foam.
5.   Add mushrooms and bamboo shoot. Reduce heat to low and simmer chicken soup for 1 hour. Season with salt. Remove to serving bowl.

(5) Fried Shredded Potatoes 炸洋芋絲

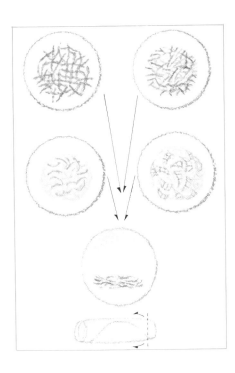

Ingredients:
2 potatoes
1 teaspoon salt
4 cups oil for deep-frying

Method:
1. Peel and shred potatoes. Soak in water with 1 teaspoon salt for 10 minutes, drain, and dry with cloth.

2. Heat 4 cups of frying oil to 375°F (190°C). Add shredded potatoes, stir and deep-fry until golden brown. (Be careful to keep potato pieces from sticking together.)

How to serve pancakes
1. Place the pancake on a plate, and spoon the filling onto the center.

2. Roll up as a sausage.

3. Fold one end to keep the oil or gravy from dripping.

4. Hold the pancake roll using the small finger to support the bottom so the gravy will stay in the roll. Bean paste is also good for filling.

III Chinese Fondue Dinner

(Serves 4 to 6)

Ingredients:
½ lb. (250 g) beef sirloin
½ lb. (250 g) fillet of sole
½ lb. (250 g) chicken breast boned
　and skinned
½ lb. shelled and deveined raw
　shrimp
1 leek

} Other kinds of meat or fish may be substituted.

A few Chinese cabbage leaves
1 onion, shredded
1 lemon
6 eggs
6 cups water
Seasoning:
　soy sauce, vinegar,
　peanut butter,
　sugar, Tabasco,
　shredded
　scallion.

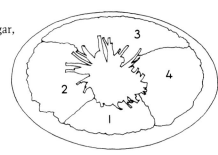

Method:
1. Put beef, sole and chicken in freezer for long enough to firm for easier slicing. Slice into the thinnest possible slices. Also cut shrimp into halves.

2. Cut two 2-inch (5 cm) lengths of leek stalks. Then cut each down half way from the end as illustrated. Drop them into cold iced water. The cut ends will spread out into flowers.

3. Arrange beef, fish, chicken and shrimp on plate and garnish with leek flowers in the center.

4. Place vegetables and eggs on another plate.

5. Use a fondue set or any other fire pot, or electric saucepan to bring water to boil.

6. Each person selects and cooks his own fish or meat on a fondue fork in hot water.

7. Raw eggs may be broken into individual bowls, stirred lightly, seasoned to taste, and used as a dip for cooked meat or fish.

8. Seasoning may be mixed in individual bowls.

9. Vegetables may be cooked after meat.

10. Lastly, you can also drink the broth remaining from the fondue.

IV Valentine Dinner (Serves 4)

(1) Tomato Rice with Shrimp 茄汁炒飯

Ingredients:

1 cup shelled raw shrimp
2 teaspoons rice wine
4 eggs
Salt and pepper
1 head broccoli
1 teaspoon salt
4 tablespoons vegetable oil

4 cups cold cooked rice
2 tablespoons tomato ketchup
4 cherries
2 tablespoons cooked green peas

Method:

1. Remove black veins from shrimp, wash in salted water and drain. Sprinkle with a dash of pepper and 2 teaspoons rice wine.

2. Beat eggs, adding a dash of salt.

3. Separate clusters of broccoli and boil in salted water. Drain.

4. Heat oil and sauté shrimp over medium heat for 1 minute. Add beaten eggs and fry until set. Remove from pan.

5. Add cold rice and tomato ketchup. Cook and stir well for 2 minutes. Return egg mixture to pan and add salt. Mix well again, remove to heated plate and arrange into heart shape.

6. Garnish with cooked broccoli and cherries around tomato rice, and form the word "valentine" with green peas.

(2) Heart Shaped Cucumber and Tomato 蕃茄黄瓜

Ingredients:

1 tomato
3 cucumbers
Salt
Seasoning:

(a) {
1 teaspoon soy sauce
1 tablespoon vinegar
1 tablespoon sesame oil
½ teaspoon salt
½ teaspoon sugar
}

Method:

1. Cut tomato into wedges.

2. Make thin slices ¾ of the way through each cucumber as illustrated.

3. Sprinkle a dash of salt on cucumbers and pull them into long strips. Arrange cucumbers and tomato as shown in photo.

4. Mix (a) in bowl and pour it over cucumbers just before serving.

V Halloween Dinner (Serves 4)

(1) Steamed Pumpkin 蒸南瓜盅

Ingredients:
1 small pumpkin or
  large acorn squash
⅓ cup diced bacon
⅓ cup diced pork
⅓ cup diced chicken meat
12 shelled and deveined
  raw shrimp
⅓ cup water
2 tablespoon rice wine
1 teaspoon salt
12 snow peas

Method:
1. Cut off top ⅕ of pumpkin to use as a "lid." Remove seeds.

2. Wash bacon, pork, chicken and shrimp in running hot water.

3. Place bacon, pork, chicken and shrimp in pumpkin with water, wine and salt.

4. Steam pumpkin in steamer with top on for 20 minutes. Add snow peas to pumpkin and steam for another 10 minutes.

(2) Stewed Pumpkin 南瓜麵塊

Ingredients:
1 small pumpkin
2 tablespoons dried shrimp
2 tablespoons rice wine
1 cup sifted flour
½ cup water
⅓ teaspoon salt
6 cups chicken stock
1 cup diced scallion
½ teaspoon salt
1 tablespoon soy sauce

Method:
1. Cut pumpkin into bite-size pieces.

2. Soak dried shrimp with 2 tablespoons wine.

3. Mix sifted flour with water. Add ⅓ teaspoon salt.

4. Bring chicken stock to boil, add pumpkin, diced scallion and soaked shrimp. Cook until pumpkin is soft.

5. Add flour mixture, 1 tablespoon at a time, to boiling pumpkin mixture. Then add ½ teaspoon salt and 1 tablespoon soy sauce. Cook for 2 minutes. Serve hot.

LUNCHEONS, SNACKS AND PASTRIES

Picnic Luncheon
Bridge Luncheon
Mahjong Snacks
Appetizers
Chinese Pastries and Coffee
Chinese Cookies and Tea

I
Picnic
Luncheon

(Serves 6)

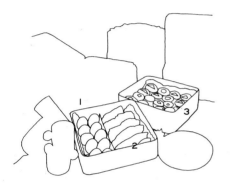

(1) Marble Eggs 茶葉蛋

Ingredients:
10 eggs
2½ cups water
3 tea bags
3 teaspoons salt
3 tablespoons soy sauce
1 star anise or ½ teaspoon
  cinnamon

Method:
1. Cover eggs with cold water and cook for 20 to 30 minutes over high heat.

2. Chill cooked eggs in cold water until cool.

3. Crack egg shells on a table or with the back of a tablespoon without removing shells.

4. Mix 2½ cups of cold water with the remaining ingredients in a saucepan. Add eggs and cook for 50 minutes over low heat. Set aside until eggs are cold.

5. Remove egg shells carefully before serving. Serve with salt or sugar as you prefer.

3   4

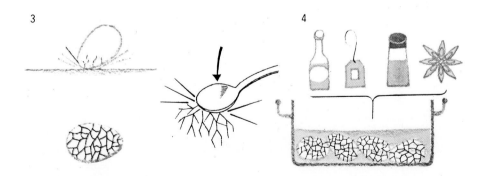

(2) Braised Chicken Wings 醬翅膀

Ingredients:
12 chicken wings

(a) {
2 cups water
4 tablespoons soy sauce
1 tablespoon sugar
1 tablespoon rice wine
}

1 green onion or scallion

1 small piece of fresh ginger, peeled, or ¼ teaspoon ginger powder

(b) {
1 tablespoon soy sauce
1 tablespoon sugar or a small piece rock candy
}

Method:

1. Wash chicken wings in running hot water and drain.

2. Mix (a) in saucepan, add chicken wings, onion and ginger. Cook over medium heat for 20 minutes.

3. Remove wings from saucepan. Add (b) to sauce and cook for 2 minutes. Then return wings to pan and cook until sauce is nearly gone. Serve cold.

(3) Picnic Rice-Ball 飯團

Ingredients:
5 cups plain hot rice

(a) {
2 tablespoons vinegar
1 teaspoon salt
}

1 piece of ham ½ inch (1 cm) thick
1 piece of cheese ½ inch (1 cm) thick
1 small cucumber

Method:

1. Mix rice well with (a).

2. Cut ham, cheese and cucumber into ½-inch (1 cm) cubes.

3. Shape rice into 15 to 16 balls, squares or triangles.

4. Press hole in the center of each rice ball and place ham, cheese or cucumber in hole.

II Bridge Luncheon (Serves 4)

(1) Barbecued Pork or Beef Rolls 义燒飽

Ingredients:
6 oz. (80 g) roast pork or beef
(a) {
2 tablespoons soy sauce
2 tablespoons sugar
1 tablespoon vegetable oil
1 tablespoon sesame oil
1 tablespoon cornstarch
}
Dough for 20 buttermilk biscuits

Method:
1. Cut roast pork or beef into ⅛ inch (3 mm) cubes.

2. Mix (a) well and cook, stirring briskly, until thickned. Add meat and mix well again. Set aside until cold.

3. Make round flat circles using two biscuits for each.

4. Put meat mixture on biscuit circles and pinch shut as illustrated, turn pinched sides down and snip a small x in the top of each roll.

5. Steam in steamer with boiling water or bake in 475°F (265°C) oven for 8 minutes.

(2) Corn Soup 粟米湯

Ingredients:
3 cups chicken stock
2 cups canned sweet corn (cream style)
2 eggs
1 tablespoon rice wine
½ teaspoon salt
1 teaspoon cornstarch, mixed with 1 tablespoon of water
1 tablespoon chopped ham and parsley

Method:
1. Bring chicken stock and sweet corn to boil. Add beaten eggs and cook for 1 minute.

2. Add rice wine, salt and cornstarch mixture. Stir well and pour into bowl. Garnish with chopped ham and parsley.

III Mahjong Snacks

(Serves 4)

(1) Chicken Rolls 鷄 捲

Ingredients:
1 cup shredded chicken breast
Seasoning:

(a) { 1 teaspoon rice wine
Salt and pepper
1 tablespoon cornstarch
1 egg white

2 cups vegetable oil
½ cup shredded celery
½ cup shredded bamboo shoots
½ cup shredded carrot

½ cup shredded leek
2 tablespoons oil
Mixture:

(b) { 1 teaspoon Tabasco
½ teaspoon salt
½ teaspoon sugar
1 teaspoon vinegar
1 teaspoon cornstarch
1 tablespoon water

16–18 thin slices very fresh
sandwich bread

Method:
1. Mix chicken with (a).

2. Heat 2 cups vegetables oil 320°F (160°C) add chicken mixture. Stir for 1 minute. Remove and drain.

3. Fry shredded celery, bamboo shoots, carrot and leek together in the same pan for 1 minute. Remove and drain.

4. Heat 2 tablespoons oil in pan. Pour (b) mixture into pan and add chicken and vegetables. Mix well.

5. Spread chicken mixture on lower third of slices of sandwich bread and roll them like a hot dog. Wrap in plastic wrap as illustrated.

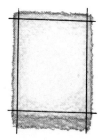   

(2) Tomato Juice 蕃茄汁

(Continued on page 113)

IV Appetizers

(Serves 4 to 6)

(1) Fried Won Ton 炸餛飩

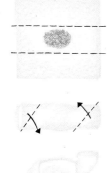

Ingredients:
1 cup shelled and deveined raw
  shrimp
1 tablespoon chopped green onion
¼ teaspoon ginger powder
(a) {
  ½ teaspoon salt
  ½ teaspoon cornstarch
  1 tablespoon sesame oil or
    salad oil
  1 tablespoon rice wine
  ¼ teaspoon pepper
}
2 dozen won ton wrappers
3–4 cups for deep-frying oil
1 tomato, sliced
¼ cucumber, sliced

Method:
1. Chop or grind shrimp.
2. Add green onion, ginger powder and (a) to shrimp. Mix well.
3. Wrap won ton as illustrated.
4. Heat oil to 375°F (190°C) for deep-frying. Fry until won ton becomes crisp and brown.
5. Garnish with tomato and cucumber.
6. Serve hot with tomato ketchup or Tabasco.

(2) Egg Rolls 蛋 捲

(Continued on page 113)

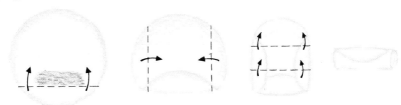

V
Chinese Pastries and Coffee

(Serves 6 to 8)

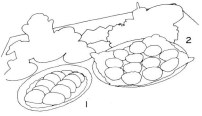

(1) Curried Meat Pies 咖喱餃

Ingredients:

Filling:
 4 tablespoons salad oil
 1 cup ground pork or beef
 1 tablespoon rice wine
 1 cup chopped onion

Mixture:

(a)
 ⅔ teaspoon sugar
 1 teaspoon salt
 1½ teaspoons curry powder
 ½ slice of bread (crumbled and soaked in 1 tablespoon water)

Pie pastry:

(b)
 2½ tablespoons lard or shortening
 2 tablespoons sugar
 4 tablespoons hot water
 1½ cups sifted flour

(c)
 1⅓ cups sifted flour
 4 tablespoons lard or shortening, softened
 2–3 tablespoons water

Method:

1. Heat 2 tablespoons oil in pan, add meat and wine, cook until meat changes color. Set aside.

2. Heat 2 tablespoons oil in pan, add onion and cook for 2 minutes or until tender. Mix with (a), stir well, add meat and mix well. Set aside until cooled.

3. (b) Mix shortening, sugar and hot water first. Then add sifted flour to make dough.

4. (c) Sift flour into shortening and stir vigorously in a circular motion, drawing dough into ball; add 2 to 3 tablespoons water if mixture will not roll into ball.

5. Roll out first (b) dough into flat circle, about 8 inches (20 cm) across, then place the ball of second dough (c) in the center and wrap in the first dough dumpling fashion.

6. Roll out again into square shape.

7. Roll up into sausage shape and cut into 10–12 sections.

8. Roll each section into a flat round piece, about 4 inches (10 cm) in diameter. Put about 1 teaspoon of meat in the center of each piece. Fold it into a halfmoon, crimping edges as illustrated (page 107).

9. Bake in hot oven at 400°F (205°C) for 12 to 14 minutes or until light brown. (Brush egg yolk on top of the pie if desired)

(2) Golden Pies 蛋　塌

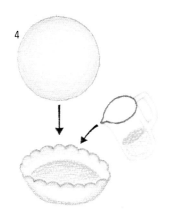

Ingredients:

2⅓ cups sifted flour

(a) {
  3½ oz. (100 g) lard or shortening
  ¼–⅓ cup hot water
  ¼ teaspoon salt
}

(b) {
  3 eggs
  1½ cups sugar
  1 cup milk
}

Method:

1.   Mix (a) well, then add sifted flour and mix again. Set aside for 30 minutes.

2.   Beat eggs of (b) well, then add sugar and milk. Remove foam with a piece of paper towel and set aside.

3.   Roll out dough mixture to ⅛ inch (3 mm) thick and cut into 12 round pieces, 3½ inches (9 cm) in diameter. Place each in a separate small tart tin. Prebake pie shell at 350°F (180°C) for 15 minutes. Set aside.

4.   Place (b) mixture in tart tins and bake in hot oven 200°F (95°C) for 6 minutes. Cover with a piece of alminium foil. Bake pie for another 2 minutes.

(continued from Curried Meat Pies)

VI Chinese Cookies and Tea

(Serves 6 to 8)

(1) Laughing Balls 開口笑

Ingredients:
1½ tablespoons lard
 or shortening
1 cup sugar
1 egg, beaten
2 cups sifted flour
2 tablespoons baking powder
¼ cup water
1 cup sesame seeds
4 or 5 cups frying oil

Method:
1.   Mix shortening and sugar for 2 minutes, add beaten egg and mix well.
2.   Pour sifted flour and baking powder into mixture (1), add ¼ cup of water a little at a time until water is used up and soft dough is formed.
3.   Roll dough into the shape of a long sausage and cut it into 30 chunks. Roll gently into balls and dip each one into sesame seeds. (If sesame does not stick to balls, you may use a little water to wet surface.)
4.   Heat frying oil to 375°F (190°C). Then reduce heat to medium and place half of balls in oil and fry until golden brown. Remove from pan and drain on absorbent paper. Fry remaining balls in the same oil.

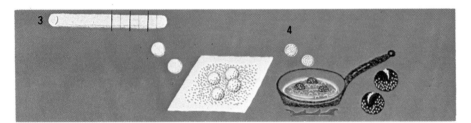

(2) Almond Cookies 杏仁酥

Ingredients:
⅔ cup lard or shortening
1⅓ cups sugar
1 egg
½ teaspoon almond extract
3–3¼ cups sifted flour
2 teaspoons baking powder
1 teaspoon soda
36 almonds

Method:
1.   Cream lard and sugar; and add egg and flavoring.
2.   Sift flour into egg mixture and blend in.
3.   Knead dough till very smooth.
4.   Form into 3 dozen small balls.
5.   Press an almond into the top of each cooky. Bake in 400°F (205°C) oven for 15 minutes.

NOTES ON CHINESE COOKING

Chinese methods of serving and hospitality

A large serving dish for each course is placed in the center of the table. Everyone helps himself using serving chopsticks or serving spoon to bring food from the serving dish to his own plate. This very informal way of serving makes for a hospitable atmosphere for the guests.

Beverages

Of course, Chinese wine goes well with Chinese food. *Shao-hsing,* a typical wine, is usually served hot, but nice to drink cold, too. Besides *Mou-tai Chiew,* Japanese wine, beer or Western wine may be served. Green tea or oolong tea is usually served to those who do not care for wine. Jasmine tea is a favorite of some people.

Table setting for a Chinese meal

The table setting is shown in the picture. A medium-sized plate for individual servings of food, a soup bowl or tea cup for soup, and chopsticks are set at each place. A bread plate may be used as a second dish for small portions of foods or for discarding chicken bones or shrimp shells. A small dish is needed for soy sauce and seasonings. Serving spoons may be required. Forks are optional and knives unnecessary since everything is cut into bite size. The napkin is placed on the plate. Salt, pepper, soy sauce and mustard are placed on the table ready to use.

SOUP BOWL OR TEA CUP
BREAD PLATE
NAPKIN
SMALL DISH
MEDIUM-SIZED PLATE

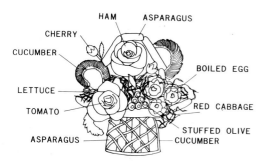

HAM   ASPARAGUS
CHERRY
CUCUMBER
BOILED EGG
LETTUCE
TOMATO
RED CABBAGE
STUFFED OLIVE
ASPARAGUS   CUCUMBER

Menu (hors d'oeuvres)

A formal Chinese dinner generally begins with a cold appetizer, followed by several hot dishes, including the soup and the sweet dish. When entertaining guests at home "one soup and four dishes" is the basic Chinese menu, but if this is not enough cold appetizers may be placed first in the center of the table as an additional dish. (See illustration.)

Foods used as hors d'oeuvres should be selected for their quality of retaining taste and color for several hours.

In China very special seafoods, meats and vegetables are served as hors d'oeuvers; however, the various items shown in the picture such as ham, boiled eggs, canned asparagus, tomatoes, red cabbage, cucumber, stuffed olives and lettuce are all very easy to obtain. Arrange these to represent flowers in a basket. In addition canned plain abalone, pickles and sausage may be served, and arranged attractively according to your taste.

When invited by a Chinese friend to his home for a meal, you can tell which kind of Chinese meal you will have by looking at the table. If the dishes to be served are all on the table, it is a family meal. The family meal will consist of at least the four basic dishes: one meat, one fish, one vegetable and one soup. You will sit down to a table setting of a bowl of rice, a pair of chopsticks, a soup bowl with a china spoon, and a plate to place your food on. You help yourself to the central dishes. At the end of the meal, hot tea will be served. Fruit or dessert may be served after the meal, but don't count on it.

If you are invited to a banquet, you should also notice the table: a banquet table must be round and is always set for ten to twelve. If more people are invited, more tables will be set. The seat farthest inside the room facing the entrance is for the guest of honor. The seats opposite the guest of honor are for the host and hostess. At a banquet, the different dishes are srved one at a time. Appetizers are first, followed by sautéed or fried dishes, then the main courses (about four to six dishes) are served. Soup and dessert may be served between the other dishes as well as the last dish. Of course, each time the soup and dessert are served, they are of different kinds.

To begin the banquet, the host drinks a toast to the guest of honor, and then the guest of honor expresses his thanks in a toast. The host then helps the guest of honor to the food. Only when the guest of honor starts to eat can the others start. So whether you are partaking of a family meal in the home of a Chinese friend or attending a banquet Chinese-style, you will always feel at home.

III Mahjong Snacks

IV Appetizers

(2) Tomato Juice
(continued from page 100)

(2) Egg Rolls
(continued from page 103)

Igredients:
1 lemon
4 cups canned tomato juice
1 teaspoon Worcestershire sauce
⅓ teaspoon salt

Method:
1. Slice 4 pieces lemon from the whole one. Make the rest lemon into juice.
2. Mix tomato juice with lemon juice. Worcestershire sauce and salt.
3. Serve the mixture in glasses and garnish with lemon slices as shown in photo.

Ingredients:

(a) {
2 eggs
2 cups milk
2 cups sifted flour
1 tablespoon oil
⅔ teaspoon salt
}
Frying oil

(b) {
1½ cups crab meat
2 tablespoons chopped green onion
1 cup chopped bamboo shoots
½ cup chopped Chinese mushrooms
1 tablespoon fresh minced ginger
⅓ teaspoon pepper
2 tablespoons sherry
1 tablespoon soy sauce
1 teaspoon sugar
1 teaspoon salt
1 teaspoon sesame oil
2 teaspoons cornstarch
}

(c) {
2 tablespoons flour
1 tablespoon water
}
3–4 cups oil for frying

Method:
1. Mix (a) well to make batter.
2. Rub oil on bottom of a small (about 6-inch., 15 cm) frying pan and heat pan for 30 seconds.
3. Pour batter into frying pan, one portion (about 2 tablespoons) at a time to make 16 pancakes.
4. Mix (b) well to make filling.
5. Wrap filling in pancakes as illustrated.
6. Mix (c) to seal pancake rolls.
7. Heat frying oil to 375°F (190°C). Deep-fry egg rolls until light brown.
8. Garnish with lettuce. Serve hot with tomato ketchup or Tabasco.

Index of Recipes

About the author:

An authority on Chinese cooking, Madame Constance D. Chang is widely known for her delicious Chinese food, her easy-to-follow-recipes, and her willingness and ability to impart her knowledge to others.

At present, Mrs. Chang owns and operates or directly supervises six Chinese restaurants in Japan. "Peacock Hall" is the name given to the three located in the Tokyo, Haneda and Yokohama Tokyu Hotels. The other three are called "Madame Chang's Home Kitchen," and are located in the Shibuya, Seijo and Hiroo districts.

Mrs. Chang has the enviable distinction of having initiated the first Chinese buffet restaurant in Japan; it is quite likely the first in the world.

She has appeared on TV cooking programs for more than 30 years and has written 14 books on Chinese cooking. She is also widely recognized for Chinese and modern paintings and calligraphy.